Jumping Gymnastics

By Ellen Labrecque

The Child's World
www.childsworld.com

Published in the United States of America by The Child's World®
1980 Lookout Drive • Mankato, MN 56003-1705
800-599-READ • www.childsworld.com

ACKNOWLEDGMENTS

The Child's World®: Mary Berendes, Publishing Director

Produced by Shoreline Publishing Group LLC
President / Editorial Director: James Buckley, Jr.
Designer: Tom Carling, carlingdesign.com
Cover Art: Slimfilms
Assistant Editor: Jim Gigliotti

Photo Credits:
Cover: Main: AP/Wide World; Insets: Corbis
Interior: AP/Wide World: 13, 23, 24, 25, 26, 27; Corbis: 12, 16;
Dreamstime.com (photographers listed): Galina Barskaya 8, 9,
David Davis 17, SportLibrary 5, 6; Reuters 7, 10, 11, 14, 15, 19,
21, 28, 29

LIBRARY OF CONGRESS CATALOG-IN-PUBLICATION DATA

Labrecque, Ellen.
  Jumping gymnastics / by Ellen Labrecque.
    p. cm. — (Reading rocks!)
  Includes bibliographical references and index.
  ISBN 978-1-60253-099-7 (library bound : alk. paper)
  1. Gymnastics—Juvenile literature. I. Title. II. Series.

GV461.3.L34 2008
796.44—dc22

                              2008004483

CONTENTS

WHAT IS
Gymnastics?

A young girl leaps like a kangaroo, high into the air. She tumbles with the speed of a fast-rolling tire. She bends her body like a rubber band. Can you guess what sort of athlete she is? She's a gymnast!

Many athletes have to be strong. Other athletes have to be fast. Others have to be **nimble**. Gymnasts have to have all these **traits** and more. They need strength to lift their own body weight. They have to be flexible to do splits and other bendy moves. They must be able to run fast and make difficult jumps. These skills make gymnasts some of the best athletes in the world.

Gymnastics is more than 2,000 years old. People in ancient Greece invented it to train soldiers. The soldiers did gymnastic moves to prepare their bodies to fight battles. Gymnastics eventually became a sport. The first world **competition** came at the 1896 Olympics in Athens, Greece. Only men were allowed to compete. Women gymnasts joined the Olympics in 1928.

Gymnasts combine great strength with beauty, balance, and grace.

This shows just how narrow the balance beam is. It's just a bit wider than a gymnast's foot.

Today, gymnastics is one of the Olympics' most popular sports. Both men and women perform in the floor exercises, which are tumbling and jumping moves on a large, square mat. They also do the **vault**. In this event, gymnasts sprint down a runway before jumping on a springy board. This launches them over the vault. They spin and flip before landing on the other side.

Women gymnasts have two special events. The wooden balance beam is only four inches (10 cm) wide and stands several feet off the floor.

Gymnasts walk, leap, somersault, and flip, all without falling off the narrow beam.

In the uneven **parallel** bars event, gymnasts flip, spin, and swoop from one bar to the other. Then they flip off the bars and soar and twist through the air before landing.

The parallel bars event demands skill and daring.

Super Carly

Carly Patterson of the United States won the all-around event at the 2004 Olympic Games. Carly was the second American woman to win the all-around gold medal. Mary Lou Retton was the first (in 1984).

Along with the vault and floor exercises, male gymnasts use three other **apparatus**.

The **pommel horse** has two wooden handles on top of it. Gymnasts use their powerful arms and shoulders to hold themselves up on these handles while doing spins and other moves.

The wooden rings hang high above the mat on stretchy ropes and cables. While dangling from these rings, gymnasts perform amazing feats of strength.

The wooden parallel bars are about five feet off the ground. Gymnasts spin, flip, and twist around on the bars before flying off.

On the rings, gymnasts try to do tricks without moving the rings too much.

Dismounts are the final tricks gymnasts perform on each apparatus. They swing or jump away with as much skill as possible. They tuck and twist—and hope to land on the ground with both feet.

Here you can see judges carefully watching a gymnast on the balance beam.

This means enthusiasm, drama, and joy expressed by the gymnast. Some athletes take drama classes to improve their scores in this area.

At gymnastics events, athletes compete on each apparatus. Judges award points for skills and form. The gymnasts must do a certain number of moves in each of their routines. They are also given points for **flair**. Judges subtract points when a gymnast falls or makes a mistake. The top score possible used to be a "perfect 10." In 2006, the gymnastics scoring system was changed. Good scores are now around 15–16 points.

In the "all-around" part of a gymnastics event, the gymnast who has the best total score wins. In the team competition, judges add the five best all-around scores of a team's members. The team with the highest score wins the competition. At the 2004 Summer Olympics, the United States women's and men's teams each won silver medals (second place)!

Second-best in the world is something for these American girls to really smile about!

The beauty and talent of gymnasts thrills fans around the world. Thanks to their Olympic success, several female gymnasts have become world superstars.

In 1972, a tiny girl named Olga Korbut charmed the world. Though very small, she could perform amazing tumbling runs and high-flying flips. And she did it all with a winning smile and cute pigtails.

Olga Korbut won hearts and a gold medal at the 1972 Olympics.

A Perfect 10

Thanks to gymnastics, the phrase "a perfect 10" means that someone has done something really well. The words first became known when Romanian gymnast Nadia Comaneci got the first score of 10 in Olympic history in 1976.

Four years later, a tall, thin athlete set a new standard. Nadia Comaneci (koh-men-EETSCH) was strong and tough, and also amazingly flexible.

Inspired by these women, America's Mary Lou Retton burst onto the scene in 1984. When she won Olympic gold in the all-around competition, her beaming smile inspired many girls to try this fun sport.

2

BECOMING A
Gymnast

U.S. gymnast Carly Patterson won three medals at the 2004 Summer Olympics. She won gold in the all-around, and silver in the team and balance-beam events. She was only 16 years old! Long before she won these medals, though, Carly knew she wanted to be a gymnast.

"I was six," Carly said. "It was at my cousin's birthday party. We got to play on the trampoline. I wouldn't stop flipping when I got home. My mom put me in gymnastics because she didn't want me to hurt myself."

Carly swung from the uneven parallel bars (opposite), and then later got a lift from her coach after winning Olympic gold in 2004.

As Carly found out, gymnastics is a fun sport for almost anyone. Do you want to become a gymnast?

The best way to get started is by contacting your local gymnastics club. Local clubs allow you to train properly. Expert coaches make sure you learn the right—and safe—way to do gymnastics.

When you first try a flip or twist, the teacher will **spot** you. This means he or she will stand next to you so you don't fall or hurt yourself. Your teacher will also show you exercises to become stronger and more flexible.

This coach is spotting a gymnast as she tries a new trick.

Most clubs split kids into groups based on age or skill levels. As you improve, you can move up into higher groups.

Attending a gymnastics summer camp is also a great way to learn the sport. There are camps all across the country. Along with regular summer-camp things such as singalongs, meals, and crafts, you do lots and lots of gymnastics. Teachers and coaches are there to help you improve your skills and learn new routines.

Joining Clubs or Camps

The Web site www.usolympicteam.com lists gymnastics clubs and camps all across the country. Ask your mom or dad to help you find the lists. The Web site www.usa-gymnastics.org also has camp and club information.

If you keep practicing your gymnastic skills, you can become good enough to compete. You can start by entering competitions in your area. Just like in the Olympics, you'll compete on various apparatus.

If you continue to improve, you can compete in state and national competitions. These are the steps it takes to reach the Olympic level. It takes a lot of work to reach the Olympics, though. Just ask U.S. gymnast Paul Hamm.

"I'm in the gym training about five hours a day," Paul says. "In the morning I go in about 11 A.M. and work out for about two and a half hours. At night I come back and work out for another couple hours."

Paul's hard work paid off. He won the all-around gold medal at the 2004 Olympic Games.

3

GOING FOR Gold!

The United States has hundreds of highly talented gymnasts. While some champion athletes are reaching the ends of their careers, others are on the rise. Here are a few rising gymnastic stars.

Shawn Johnson has become a favorite of gymnastics fans. This talented teen won the all-around gold medal at the 2007 World Championships. She also won gold in the floor-exercise competition.

Along with gold medals, Shawn won a thank-you hug from her coach, Liang Qiao.

"It feels unreal," Shawn said about winning her two big titles. "I never saw it coming. I never pictured any of this."

Shawn has been a natural gymnast since she was a baby. At nine months old, she climbed out of her crib! "I think I was born a monkey," she said.

Shawn grew up in Iowa. Her energy and strength, along with a lot of hard work, led her quickly into the top levels of young gymnasts. She worked her way up from local competitions to win state titles.

By 2006, she was traveling the world taking part in competitions. Shawn

Shawn does a back handspring on the balance beam, showing off her strength and flexibility.

joined U.S. teams in Belgium, Hawaii, Canada, Ireland, and Brazil. "Being able to see new places is one of my favorite things about gymnastics," says Shawn.

In February 2007, Shawn won the U.S. National Championships. That big win gave her a spot on the U.S. team in the World Championships in Germany— another trip for Shawn!

As the 2007 world champion, Shawn earned a trip to the 2008 Olympics.

Going into the final event, the floor exercises, Team U.S.A. trailed the team from China. But Shawn and her teammates flipped and flew higher and better than the Chinese . . . and the United States became the world champion!

Nastia's long legs give her a graceful, elegant look on the beam.

One of Shawn's teammates was Nastia Liukin. She was the U.S. all-around champion in 2005 and 2006. Along with her team championship, Nastia won the gold medal in the balance beam event.

Nastia has gymnastics running through her blood. Her dad, Valeri, won four medals at the 1988 Olympics. He competed for his **native** country, the Soviet Union (now called Russia). Nastia's mom, Anna, won the 1987 world title in rhythmic gymnastics (see page 29).

"I love running into my parents' old friends who are still a part of gymnastics," Nastia says. "I feel like part of a big family."

Alicia Sacramone is another gymnast to keep your eye on. Alicia competes for her college team, Brown University, as well as for the United States. At the 2007 World Championships, she won a silver medal on the floor exercise and a bronze medal (third place) on the vault.

Three cheers for the red, white, and blue . . . and for U.S. star Alicia Sacramone.

America's male gymnasts are also among the world's best. Leading the way on the men's team are David Durante, 28, and Alexander Artemev, 23. They led the United States to a fourth-place finish at the 2007 World Championships.

At the 2007 U.S. Championships, David won the gold medal in the

Alexander shows his skills on the parallel bars. The white chalk on his hands helps him keep a good grip on the bars.

all-around, while Alexander won the silver. David is a graduate of Stanford University. He says he got into gymnastics after his parents got tired of him jumping on the furniture! Alexander's dad, Vladimir, and his mom, Svetlana, were gymnasts who competed for the Soviet Union.

Paul Hamm, the 2004 Olympic champ, is still competing. Paul's amazing gold-medal performance at the 2004 Olympics was one of the sport's great success stories. He won by .0012 points. It was the closest Olympic gymnastics finish ever! In 2003, he became the first American world champion, too.

David Durante concentrates as he holds a pose on the rings.

Here's Wei Yang hitting the vault on his way over. You can see his powerful arms pushing him into the air.

American gymnasts face tough competition from around the world. At the 2007 World Championships, the Chinese women finished second, while the Chinese men came in first. The year before, both of China's teams won world titles.

Powerful and graceful Wei Yang of China is the top male gymnast in the world. He didn't win any individual medals at the 2007 world event, but his combined scores made him the all-around champion.

On the women's side, Romania's Steliana Nestor finished second to Shawn Johnson at the World Championships in 2007. Three Chinese women won medals in individual events, too.

No matter who wins medals, gymnasts will always enjoy competing. It's time for you to jump into gymnastics!

Other Ways to Perform

Here are two other types of gymnastics.

Rhythmic Gymnastics: These gymnasts use ribbons (right), hoops, and balls while performing floor exercises.

Trampoline Gymnastics: Gymnasts jump on a trampoline and perform somersaults and twists in the air.

GLOSSARY

apparatus equipment designed for a special purpose—in this case, for gymnastics

competition a contest

dismounts in gymnastics, dismounts are the final tricks gymnasts do as they leave an apparatus

flair in gymnastics, flair is the extra drama and enthusiasm added to basic tricks

native the place where a person was born

nimble quick and light in movement

parallel objects (in this case, bars) that run alongside one another and never cross

pommel horse an apparatus with handles that male gymnasts use by lifting or pushing with their arms while swinging their legs

spot to watch or assist an athlete in order to prevent injury

traits qualities or features

vault an apparatus that gymnasts run toward and leap over while doing various tricks; gymnasts are able to leap over a vault with help from a springboard.

FIND OUT MORE

BOOKS

Gymnastics
By Christin Ditchfield (Grolier's Children's Press, 2000)
A young reader's guide that touches lightly on everything in gymnastics.

The Gymnastics Book
By Elfi Schlegel and Claire Ross Dunn (Firefly Books, 2001)
This book covers everything about the sport, including stories about some of its stars.

I Love Gymnastics
By Naia Bray-Moffatt (DK Books, 2005)
Follow a group of young gymnasts as they learn basic techniques and moves.

WEB SITES

Visit our Web site for lots of links about gymnastics:
www.childsworld.com/links

Note to Parents, Teachers, and Librarians: We routinely check our Web links to make sure they're safe, active sites—so encourage your readers to check them out!

INDEX

ELLEN LABRECQUE is a former editor at *Sports Illustrated for Kids*, where she wrote about basketball, gymnastics, skateboarding, and many other sports. She has also written several other books on sports for young readers. She lives in New Jersey with her husband (who's also a writer!) and her two children.